Fallen from a Tree

Joseph Drda

ISBN 978-1-0980-6711-3 (paperback)
ISBN 978-1-0980-6712-0 (digital)

Christian Faith Publishing, Inc.
832 Park Avenue
Meadville, PA 16335
www.christianfaithpublishing.com

Printed in the United States of America

Introduction

As I write my book, *Fallen from a Tree*, I reflect on my life and my parents and my family. We often struggled financially, yet we learned the importance of God and family in our lives. I've discovered many things in life that people take for granted. I've always enjoyed sports and being outside. I enjoyed being out in the woods and seeing wildlife. I was fortunate enough to have a dad who taught us sports and games where we would track our family in the snow.

I enjoyed hearing hunting stories from my dad, Uncle Gary, and Uncle Steve. I often went small game hunting with my dad and Uncle Gary using me like a dog to flush rabbits or grouse. My uncle Gary took me on my first hunt when I was twelve years old because my dad had to work.

My neighbor Jim Potts took me to my hunter safety course when I was twelve. He took me hunting in the evening after work and when I got out of school. My uncle Steve got me interested in fishing, trapping, and my favorite thing to do, archery hunting.

I had good mentors to teach me the safety use of and respect for firearms. They got me started on hunting at a young age. I expanded my knowledge by reading outdoor magazines, like *Pennsylvania Game News*, *Outdoor Life*, *Field & Stream*, *Archery World Magazine*, and *Bowhunter Magazine*.

After I finished college at Slippery Rock University, I had more time to really study wildlife in their natural environment. I became a very good turkey hunter, shooting three turkeys with my bow. I became a better deer hunter because of archery hunting and trapping where I spent more time in the woods.

From a young age, we were taught about God. We prayed as a family together at night. We were taught the importance of the Ten

Commandments in our lives and to always tell the truth. It was good that God blessed me with good parents.

You as a person don't know when God will call your name. I had no clue that I would fall from my tree stand on October 3, 2018. I sustained five broken ribs and a bad bruise on my right knee. I wasn't supposed to die on October 5, 2018. God's plan had changed my life to make it even better for my faith and to trust in Him.

I discovered that God gave us many gifts that we often take for granted. I never realized that things we learned to do in our lives that were second nature to us could eventually become so difficult. I learned to appreciate people with physical or mental handicaps even more. I became that person who was physically changed. I had to how-to-do things—such as talking, walking, eating, and drinking—all over again.

I saw how constipation could change our mood and our sleep patterns. I learned to appreciate people who had a long-term illness, such as heart problems, cancer, kidney problems, or any other health-related illnesses.

When I was in pain and was suffering from a long, grueling day in bed, I thought of Jesus suffering on the cross for our sins. How compassionate and loving He was to give His life for us that if we honor and love Him, we can join Him in everlasting life. He will keep His promise to us if we obey, love, and honor Him!

Fallen from a Tree

Today is November 3, 2018. It's been a month now since my heart took an incredible journey of reflection in my life with God. I didn't have a notebook until yesterday. My notebook was my heart and mind as well as God's guidance. After all, God spoke to me, and He revealed Himself to me, and I answered Him. It's impossible that it was just a dream. I am God's humble servant. I am not a prophet or a false god. I never in my life expected to be God's servant in such a beautiful way!

My mom, Mary, and my dad, Robert, were very good Catholic parents. My mom and dad were married on August 11, 1956. My dad was a carpenter, and our family grew up in a loving Christian environment although we often struggled financially.

My mom had kidney problems when she was twenty-six years old. She had one kidney removed because it failed. Doctors told her that she wouldn't be able to have children because either she would die or the children would die or both. My mom loved children and really wanted them. She was very devastated by the doctor's words.

My mom often told my sister, brothers, and I that we were all miracles. My mom became pregnant after she was married, but after two months, she had a miscarriage. She baptized the baby. She often said that we had a brother or sister in heaven. After her miscarriage, she was afraid that she may never have children. She said she went to a priest and talked about the fear of becoming pregnant. Mom prayed to God that she would have children, not trusting the doctors but worried.

She became pregnant again, and my sister Frances was born on November 24, 1957. Maybe the doctors were right, but obviously they were wrong! Other miracles in our family followed. I was born on February 20, 1959, fifteen months after my sister. My brother Michael was born less than a year later on February 19, 1960. I often made jokes with Michael about putting my mom in the hospital on my first birthday and sent him cards about it. You see, back then, mothers stayed in the hospital for nine days. Just think how traumatic that would be to a little child. Charles was born on July 14, 1961. Christopher was born on January 20, 1964. My youngest brother, Thomas, was born on March 17, 1968. For a lady who was told by doctors she wouldn't have children, the miracles happened by the power of God!

As very young children, my mom and dad already instilled Christian values within our family. In our family, the order of importance was this: (1) God, (2) family, and (3) work. My father, Robert, was a carpenter. At a young age, my father taught us about the importance of God and work.

I remember the first time I went to church with my dad without the rest of the family. I really wanted to go to church with him. We went together, and he sat beside me. I was very comfortable until he left me. I became very nervous. I wondered where he went in the great crowd of people at Our Lady, Queen of the Americas at Conneaut Lake, Pennsylvania. My uncle Steve must have been very close by and sensed my nervousness and anxiety of being alone. He came and sat beside me, and I felt much better and relieved.

At age ten, I was an altar boy. Monsignor Toland was the priest at our church. After mass, we would kneel, and he would give us altar boys a blessing. Father Spiece was a priest during the summer at our church. I liked him very much, and he was a good priest. Later when I was an adult, I had him as priest again.

One summer day, I served in four masses. I worked with my dad to remodel our church. The plan was to help installing aluminum siding, then I would leave prior to mass to serve again. After serving the fourth mass, Father Spiece said, "Joseph, if you died today, you will go directly to heaven." Little did I know that his prediction would come true, for it is written, "You don't know the time or the hour of death." It's true. I didn't know that I would die so soon.

I love to hunt, especially using archery! I like to hunt deer and turkeys with a bow and arrow. I have shot three turkeys with the bow. As a young child, I went with my dad to help him do carpenter work and learned how to remodel houses and fix roofs by putting new shingles on them. I learned the importance of climbing from a young age. I often climbed trees to the top. I wasn't afraid of heights as long as I knew I could safely come down. When I was ten years old, I remember climbing on a roof to give my dad tools or carry some shingles. My dad said it was thirty feet up to the roof.

As a young child, I was fascinated with climbing trees. I challenged myself to climb to the top or as high as possible. The higher I climbed, the greater my sense of accomplishment was. I didn't have any fear of heights as long as I knew I could safely get down. I often climbed trees to pick apples or pears for my family, and my dad would catch them as I dropped them down to fill a basket. I climbed trees to archery-hunt long before tree stands were popular and our family could buy one.

My 2018 bowhunting season opened with high expectations. For the first time in my life, I started the archery season in the Pittsburgh area, which had the season opened up two weeks earlier than our part of Pennsylvania. My good friend Dana Kelly wanted to hunt with me, giving me more motivation to want to go. We scouted the area for a couple of weekends prior to the season.

The second weekend of scouting revealed an abundance of white oak acorns. White oak acorns can be a very good food source to hunt near. It was raining very hard when we were scouting, yet the deer signs of buck rubs, big tracks, and droppings nearby were encouraging. Dana and I chose our places to hunt. We hunted from the ground.

The first day of archery season arrived on September 15, 2018. As the sun was rising, I heard the continuous sound of the white acorns falling. I was hoping that I could at least harvest a white-tailed doe. At sunrise, a couple of turkeys started calling. They were very close to my location. I knew that I would be seeing them when the turkeys flew from their roosting tree. I gave them a few clucks from my mouth. I learned to do clucks and yelps with my mouth. I even learned how to call deer and owl-hoot with my mouth. I believe that calling to wildlife with my mouth enhances the hunt and makes it more enjoyable to communicate with animals in nature. Even though it wasn't turkey season, I enjoyed observing turkeys and other wildlife to pass the time while on stand waiting for a deer.

It was very warm, and the mosquitoes must have opened their hunting season that day also. It was difficult to sit still with swarming mosquitoes buzzing in my ears and biting me. It was very hot in the evening hunt. Dana and I went to eat lunch, and I bought a Thermacell to help repel the mosquitoes. I saw woodchucks and a couple of squirrels coming by to eat acorns. Since it was so hot, I figured the deer would probably not move until near dark.

Dana and I set up a couple of trail cameras during the afternoon. From the number of buck rubs in the area, I believed that we would get pictures of a nice buck. About twenty minutes before quitting time, two does walked in about thirty yards away. The second doe in line spotted me on the ground in front of them, causing them to become nervous. They walked back and forth, stomped their feet, and bobbed their heads. It's the white-tailed deer's way of using body language to indicate that they suspected danger to signal other deer. Eventually, the deer walked away as darkness descended and the hunting hours ended.

The following Saturday, we hunted again. Dana and I were excited about the day. The day brought cooler weather, and we anticipated better deer movement for the day. We checked the trail cameras, and they contained several pictures of big bucks. The bucks were nocturnal, yet we had hopes that one would wander by during hunting hours. We didn't see any deer during the day hunting.

On September 29, 2018, the first day of archery season arrived in my deer management area. I was excited to be starting the hunting season closer to home. I had several very nice bucks in the trail cameras all summer and early fall, but I didn't see any deer in the morning.

I chose my Timber Tall tree stand for the evening hunt. I had been getting trail camera pictures of a very nice buck. The deer was usually moving by the stand early, sometimes close to three hours before quitting time. I climbed up a tree that would put me within fifteen yards of a good deer trail. I was about twenty-one feet off the ground. I was very well-camouflaged by the leaves in the tree I was in and the one beside me. The wind was very light, and I believed it was in favor to avoid detection from the whitetail's nose.

I was sitting down for almost an hour high above the ground. I watched squirrels gathering acorns to pass the time. I had a squirrel climb up the tree next to me, eating an acorn. I enjoy watching wildlife in its natural environment. A little while later, it was very quiet and peaceful. I was startled by the noise of a tree about as big as my forearm that I couldn't see behind me shaking. I slowly turned around to see the tree shaking, but I didn't see anything around it. I wondered what had happened. Maybe it was a raccoon because a squirrel wasn't big enough to shake the tree.

I didn't see anything, but the tree stopped shaking. About five seconds later, I looked down right under the tree stand on my left side, spotting a very nice, big eight-point buck with close to a twenty-inch antler spread. I slowly picked up my bow, waiting for a good shot. The shot would have been straight down and probably not an advisable shot. I patiently waited as he slowly walked away as I readied for a shot. At about eight yards, he stopped. He slowly started to quarter away, anticipating a shot. I suddenly heard a truck coming down the road. I made one mistake that I didn't think was going to be a problem. My choice of stand was only fifty yards off the dirt road. The buck looked up toward the approaching truck, and I drew my bow. Unfortunately, the truck hit a bump, and the deer, spooked, ran back into the woods from the direction he came. He stopped about forty yards behind me and behind some brush, making a shot impossible. I don't like to shoot from more than thirty yards. I thought he might come back down the trail again, and since the season was just starting, I figured I would see this buck again sometime. I experimented with a couple of buck grunts, and he stood calmly. I watched as he walked away.

After working on October 3, 2018, I went bowhunting. I started climbing my tree stand with a seat climber without a safety harness. I was an National Bowhunter Education instructor. We taught students to use a safety harness. I felt safe with my Timber Tall tree stand using the seat climber. I found out that not using a safety harness was a mistake. I began climbing the tree stand that I previously set up Monday after work while hunting. I climbed twenty-one feet using this tree stand Saturday night. I climbed to approximately twenty feet and left the stand in the woods for my next hunt. Because it rained Tuesday night, I had to wait. As I was going higher in climbing the tree stand, I got stuck on a knot on the tree. I got stuck on this knot Monday night also. I usually go around a knot by moving the stand around to the tree to right. Suddenly, I heard a snap, and I was falling backward headfirst toward the ground. I couldn't see the ground! Quickly, I remembered the diving I learned as a young boy and teenager from diving boards at swimming pools and even our family pond. I often did back dives and summersaults into the water from our diving platforms twelve and seventeen feet high. I tucked my head and curled my back, then landed on my shoulder blades. I hit the ground very hard, knocking the wind out of me. I couldn't breathe and tried desperately to breathe again. I remembered from my athletic training class at Slippery Rock University to pretend to whistle. I wasn't sure what would happen. I thought, *Will I even breathe again and possibly pass out?*

I struggled to move with the top part of the tree stand (the tree seat) around me. I moved so I could reach in my jacket pocket to pull out my phone. The phone only had 5 percent battery life left. I worried because at 5 percent, the battery often went dead very quickly. It's ironic. Today is November 6, 2018, as I write this. Four days ago, my friend Chuck Larsen told me on the phone that the doctors only gave me a 5 percent chance of living. I was fortunate to be able to call my friend Jerrod Dean.

I said, "Jerrod, I have a problem!"

Jerrod said, "What?"

I said, "I fell from my tree stand!"

He said, "No! You didn't."

I said, "You need to come find me!" Jerrod knew where I lived. I often hunted with him.

Jerrod said, "Joe, I have to pick up my daughter."

My battery was almost dead. I almost panicked! I called my friend Rick Uplinger. I was afraid he might be archery hunting! Rick also knew where I lived and might be able to find me. Rick said, "I'll be right over!" I gave him short directions on where to find me. As it turned out, Jerrod called. He said his daughter was with him now, and he was on his way over. Jerrod arrived to my home quickly. While waiting, I worked myself free from the seat climber that surrounded my chest and back. I used the seat climber as a place to sit down and wait for my help to arrive.

Jerrod called me on the phone. He walked through the woods and owl-hooted. It's a skill I taught him. I was less than half a mile away. I hooted back on this calm day, yet Jerrod couldn't hear me. Crazy! A couple of springs ago, Jerrod was scouting turkeys near my home. He called me on the phone. It was a cold, frosty, very still morning. Jerrod said, "Did you just owl-hoot? I think I just heard you." Jerrod was at least a mile and a half away.

Jerrod continued talking on the phone as he was trying to locate me. I told him to follow a path and that he should be able to come within fifteen yards of me. Jerrod arrived, and I told him my glasses were on the ground. He found them for me. Rick, Jake, and Joe arrived to help. I sat on my tree seat, using it as a chair by placing it sideways on the ground. Jerrod called to my friends Rick, Jake, and Joe to guide them with their voice to me. Jerrod, Jake, and Joe walked out ahead of Rick and me. I couldn't have anyone touch me because I was in severe pain.

I asked, "Rick, what vehicle did you drive?"

Rick said, "Jake drove."

I said to Rick, "Have Jim Zill come pick me up. I won't be able to get in his truck." I already had a difficult time getting into Jake's truck even before my accident.

Walking out of the woods was very difficult. I was about half a mile away from my house. I told Rick to call Jake to bring my lawn tractor to the edge of the field below my house. I rode the lawn tractor up to my house to avoid some of the walking. I rode it for about 150 yards. It took about two hours for me to get out of the woods.

Rick helped me into Jim's car. It was a very slow process to move my body to sit down on the seat. It was extremely painful to bend my head to get into the car while trying to protect my ribs while sitting down. He helped me lift my sore leg into the car, which seemed very stiff.

Rick attempted to move the seat by leaning it backward. He leaned it back too far, and I began yelling in intense pain. "Lift it up! Lift it up! Oh! It hurts!" Rick moved the seat forward and went too far, causing me to lean forward. I yelled again from the pain. Rick apologized, finally adjusting the seat in the correct position.

Jim started the car and drove to the hospital. He drove slowly, trying to avoid the bumps on my rough dirt road. I felt every bump, curve, and turn vibrate through my upper body.

We arrived at the hospital, and Jim went inside first to get somebody to help me into the wheelchair that was brought out. It was a difficult challenge to get into the wheelchair while trying to avoid as much pain as possible. I went to the hospital on October 3, 2018, for a CAT scan and X-rays. It was discovered that I had five broken ribs. I was very lucky that I didn't puncture my lungs with those five broken ribs.

I don't remember too much about October 4th. I stayed in the hospital overnight and slept a lot that day. I was very exhausted and sore from the fall. I called to tell my employer that I probably won't be able to work for a few days. On October 5th, I talked to my brother Michael. I seemed to be relaxed but extremely sore in my back and ribs.

As I Died

My brother Michael was sitting with me as the nurse walked out of the room. I started coughing almost immediately as she passed through the doorway. Michael said, "Cough it up, Joe! Cough it up, Joe!" My ribs hurt from a very intense pain as I coughed, and my back in the shoulder blades area of the ribs then seemed to vibrate in my sternum in front of my ribs. I kept coughing and started to become dizzy and felt as if I would pass out. I remember pointing to the door and falling backward as my brother ran to get the nurse.

I don't remember anything after this except that everything suddenly went black! I was looking up at the ceiling from my bed as I had an oxygen mask put on by the medical team. I was on the bed down the hallway, being pushed by the medical staff. Originally, I saw people around me, and I could hear them talking. Something changed! Suddenly, the ceiling started spinning, similar to that scene from *The Wizard of Oz*! There was a green-white, green-white spinning like a tornado similar to a green-white, green-white kaleidoscope as I described it. I said, "God, if I did anything wrong, please forgive me!" I continued to travel through this tornado-like area. Things continued spinning and became very distorted. It looked like distorted people were around me. I remember my garbled voice saying, "I'm going with God! I'm going with God! I'm going with God! I'm going with God!"

I continued seeing the spinning motion as I climbed higher. Colors changed as I went straight up. Things became clearer but darker and iridescent! I looked around to the right and to the left. Suddenly looking to the left, I saw the most handsome man I ever saw in my life! He had long dark hair tight to his face, just past his shoulders. He had a red robe tight to his body all the way to his

13

feet. He was about twenty-five yards away, walking toward me. I saw him for approximately seven seconds. I thought, *Wow! There's God, and He's wearing my favorite color! He is coming to greet me!* He motioned for me to come to Him using his fingers as if to say "Come to me" as he continued walking toward me! I said, "God, why aren't you talking to me?" Things changed, and He became very peculiar. I began to have a strange feeling that something wasn't right about this man that I saw on my left.

I yelled, "Devil, I'm going with God!" I pointed to heaven, away from the devil and upward. It was as if I was a magician! The devil vanished right before my eyes in a puff of smoke! It was my last test, my last temptation. The devil had tried to trick me into believing that he was God.

I started rising higher in my hospital bed, seeing different colors from gray to lighter, brighter colors. Suddenly, it was as if I was in a baby basket. The bed disappeared, and my feet were close. I was about three feet tall. My pain disappeared! I had zero pain! I was pain free! I believe that at that moment, I had died! I became like a child! Matthew 18:3 said, "Truly I tell you, unless you change and become like little children, you will never enter the Kingdom of Heaven."

I began thinking of my mom. On the day of her funeral, I said, "If mom isn't in heaven, we are all in trouble!" I called, "Mom, where are you?"

I heard my mom's voice! "Joseph, I am over here!"

Wow, I just heard my mom! Being a turkey hunter, I knew I was close. I rose higher and higher! Colors changed into brighter colors. I got a short glimpse of heaven, almost like a clear, bright sunrise. I could see forever! It seemed like there were small mountains off in the distance. Heaven was so beautiful! I was thinking of my mom. I should be closer now! I called, "Mom, where are you?"

She responded, "Joseph, I am over here!"

I was thinking about a reason to go back to Earth. I was thinking my family—sister, brothers, relatives—wouldn't know what happened to me. My feeling now, my mind was being read by God. I heard God's voice! He said, "Is there any reason you want to go back to earth?"

I said, "My family won't know what happened to me." Wow! I am going to see God and my mom at the same time!

God said, "Do you want to go back?"

I said, "Yes!"

Within a second, I heard, "Joe, Joe, wake up! Are you okay?" I opened my eyes, and I was with about twenty doctors and nurses. I received two more broken ribs from CPR that was started by a nurse. I remember when I was attending CPR training class, the instructor said that if it is done correctly, you could break ribs while administering it. I now had a total of seven broken ribs. I died from blood clots breaking off from the bruise on my right knee and lodging into my heart and lungs. I had been dead for six and a half minutes.

I spoke to my brother Michael about what happened to me later. He was the first one whom I told about going to heaven. I asked him what had happened to me after he went to get the nurse. He said that he ran out to get the nurse who just left. When they got back to the room, my face and skin were navy blue already. The nurse called out a code and started CPR on me. She told my brother to go get another nurse. As the code was called, medical staff came running to the room to give me assistance.

In May 2019, I went to a pig roast/gun raffle at Norrisville Sportsman's Club. I saw my friend Steve Folmar and spoke to him about my near-death experience. At the raffle, near Steve, I saw a lady who had a T-shirt that had *God* and *Trump* written on it. I told her I liked her shirt. I told her, "Believe it or not, I died and went to heaven."

She said, "So did I!" She was getting up to go smoke a cigarette, and I asked her if I could come back to listen to her story. I went back to talk to her later. Her name was Dottie. She told me that she had a near-death experience in November 2018. She was having her lungs operated on and died. She said she saw a bright light, then saw her mom. Dottie said that her mom said, "It's not your time! Go back!" She said that, similar to me, she came back in about a second. Then something very amazing happened! I needed some inspiration as I was trying to write more to share with others in my book. I was at a standstill, wanting to write something new and inspirational. I started telling her about my story and how my brother told me the nurse called out a code for assistance for me. She asked, "Did that happen in October?"

I said, "Yes."

She said, "I was on that code, watching the monitors for vitals!"

Her job was to watch the vitals closely, and she concentrated mostly on her job. I asked her if she knew anything about what happened as the doctors and nurses worked to revive me. She said that I was navy blue, the color of the shirt she was wearing, and my lips were black. She said that I was in a very dangerous situation because I already had broken ribs. She said the doctors used a defibrillator to get my heart started again. She said my body was jumping off the bed as she described the team working on me.

Wow! How amazing that I would meet a member of the medical team that worked on me. I believe it was a sign from God to help encourage me to continue working on the assignment that He had given to me to write and speak about my incredible journey. It seemed to me that to find a lady who was a nurse on that emergency situation was as likely as finding a needle in a haystack or winning the lottery. God really blessed me with this miracle gift to encourage me that He watches over me to come to my aid when I pray for help. I had prayed for God to come to my assistance. Thank you, God, for your great gift and encouragement.

On November 2, 2018, almost a month from the day when I fell out of the tree stand, my friend Chuck Larson told me that the doctors in UPMC Presbyterian said I only had 5 percent chance to live. I said, "Really? God gave me 100 percent!"

I believe that God revealed to me a mission. I was to write a book and speak to others about God and heaven. I was to be a spokesman that God and heaven are real. I suddenly had the desire to be able to speak in churches and lectures about my experience in going to heaven.

Today is April 16, 2019. I have often asked people if they wanted to hear my story. One day, I thought, *This story isn't mine.* It was a story written about me with God as the author. I had been falling headfirst and couldn't see the ground. I could have died in my fall from the tree stand, but I tucked my chin to land on my shoulder blades. I broke five ribs and had a bruise on my knee. I could have broken bones in my legs, arms, head, or spine. I could have easily been paralyzed for the rest of my life. God protected me for a purpose. I needed to be in the hospital with a non-life-threatening injury. I had to have a medical team revive me after I died; otherwise, this story would not be valid. God gave me this opportunity to reveal that He is the truth!

I wrote seven children's stories that I never got published. They were stories with rhymes that had some humor and educational value. My mom said, "Those are funny, and you are a good writer, but you need to write a serious story." Well, Mom, I guess I am writing a serious book now!

The Blues Brothers was one of my favorite movies. Dan Akroyd and John Belushi played Elwood and Jake Blues. My new theme in life is, "We're on a mission from God!"

Well, after I returned from heaven, my pain returned. I guess it was God's way of making me do penance for my sins! Unfortunately, everyone has sinned. Nobody is perfect but God! As a small child, I remember finding money in the closet. I was about six years old. My neighbor told me that if I gave him the money, he would get me a cowboy hat and a cap gun like he had. We were a very poor family. I didn't know that I was stealing. The money was my dad's garden fund. I guess money doesn't come from heaven when you find it.

My mom taught me to always tell the truth at a young age. Although I always tried my best, I avoided revealing some things in order to not hurt others' feelings. Sometimes, it seems that people didn't like hearing the truth, so I remained silent.

I had some doubts about God's plan for me. My doubts in God were that, although I loved children and working with them, I never got married and had children and never got a permanent teaching job. I thought I would be a good husband and father. I enjoyed teaching and coaching teenagers and children. I often found the few ladies I dated to be dishonest to me. I didn't choose to date them for looks but what was in their heart.

The other doubt was that my mother always prayed for me to get a teaching job. I tried very hard as a substitute teacher in three school districts—Conneaut, Penncrest, and Crawford Central School District. I coached football, volleyball, basketball, and softball.

Children really enjoyed having me teach them. They often told me that I was their favorite teacher. I had a former girl student who told me through Facebook that I was her favorite teacher. I coached my friend Jerrod in football. Later, he was in the group that helped me get out of the woods. It took two hours to get out of the woods from the time I fell out of the tree stand, then walked about half a mile. Jerrod told me that I really motivated him as a coach. His boss, Doug Peters, was my assistant girls basketball coach. I went to talk to Jerrod and Matt Lojek, a former student and football player I coached, who were Doug's employees. I was planning to turkey-hunt in New York. Matt and Jerrod were also planning to hunt in New York. Jerrod and Matt had previously gone to a game lands to scout. Jerrod and I went to the area we scouted. We heard gobbling; however, the gobblers went to the opposite side of the field. The next Sunday (No, I didn't miss churchgoing on Saturday night), we set up on the opposite side. The turkeys went to the side we were previously on.

Jerrod and I hunted archery deer and rifle deer hunting together. In 2016, Jerrod bought a beagle to rabbit-hunt. His beagle's name was Molly. Jerrod told me that I should buy a beagle. He found a beagle online. I went to pick him out. The grandfather in the beagle's bloodline was national champion. His father was very good with champion bloodlines.

I named my dog Thor. He was the third beagle I ever had. My friend Rick and his daughter Brittany took care of him when I was hospitalized. Thor suddenly became the leader of the pack when chasing rabbits at high velocity with other beagles. He would pass other dogs as if they were standing still! I named him as I registered him for American Kennel Club (AKC) Thor Hillview Locomotive. Hillview is the road I live on. I call him a heathen because he would always get into garbage and use the house as his bathroom. I told my friends Rick and Jim that when I got out of the hospital, I was going to baptize him with holy water! Years ago, my mom went to a religious retreat at Sainte-Anne's in Canada. She met a man whom she continued talking to. He often prayed with his dog leading the way to the prayer room. He told my mom that *dog* is *God* spelled backward. Dogs can definitely be a man's best friend.

Good things developed because of my friendship with Jerrod and other students. I was truly blessed to have great friends. Many memories will last forever!

It was time to get better in the hospital. I asked for a Catholic priest named Father Lucas at Meadville Medical Center. I asked him to give me last rites after I told him my story about dying and going to heaven and talking to God. I confessed my sins to him! My sins were small. Technically, God had forgiven me already; otherwise, I wouldn't have been here talking to the priest. I also told my story to my family doctor, Dr. Martin Decker.

I was life flighted in a helicopter form Meadville Medical Center some time after I received medical care from the doctors and nurses. I thanked them for their efforts to revive me, but God gave me the choice to live or die! He gave me a special gift that wasn't revealed to me until I was able to talk. My brother Michael was sitting by me. I said, "Remember that you died and had an out-of-body experience when you had spinal meningitis? I had one also!" I told him what happened. I believe that he was amazed. Later, I told my sister, Frances, and my niece Amy. Frances told me later that she thought I was lying until she looked into my eyes, then she knew I was telling the truth!

Weeks later, Frances talked to me with a nurse named Sue at UPMC Presbyterian that she and Amy told many people about my experience. Wow! She made me so extremely happy! Sue told me in the morning that another man had a similar experience. She thought the man was still in the hospital. I was hoping that I could meet him. When she checked, he had left the day before. She told Frances and me about what happened in the evening. The man had an artery cut and died. God reached down His hand and pulled him back. God told him to make up with his son who he hadn't talked to in about two years.

I was transferred to Hamot hospital in Erie, Pennsylvania, life flighted on a helicopter. Being moved from the hospital bed was very painful to my chest and back because I had CPR given to me after five broken ribs, so I had two more for a total of seven.

At Hamot, I had visits from my brother Michael and his son Walter, my sister, Frances, and my friends Bob Smith and Randall Stevenson. It was Sunday, and I watched the Pittsburgh Steelers game.

Monday, October 8, 2018, was Columbus Day. It was my friend Rick Uplinger's birthday. My brother Michael called my friend Rick to tell him that I died again. Rick said, "No! Joe can't die on my birthday!" Months later, Rick told me that my brother called him and said the doctor told him to call in the whole family because I probably wasn't going to make it through the night. I told Rick that we shared the same birthday now! I knew that I had died once but didn't realize that I was so close to death a second time.

I told my brother Michael later that I had a second near-death experience. I told him that I saw him through a window in the hospital. He said, "That's impossible!" He told me that it was impossible for me to see him. He went into a waiting room with a window on it facing the hallway. I responded, "I wasn't in that part of the hospital, but I saw you there!" In this experience, I told the doctor that I wasn't going to die as he was working on me.

I was prepared for ECMO at Hamot. It was one of the first times that this procedure was done there. ECMO stands for extracorporeal membrane oxygenation and is a life-support machine. ECMO is used on infants and adults who have a severe life-threatening illness that stops the heart and lungs from working properly.

I was life-flighted to UPMC Presbyterian in Pittsburgh, Pennsylvania, by a helicopter for my second helicopter ride. I only remember bits and pieces of it.

I was in an induced coma for seven days. I believe I had many nightmares while I was in an induced coma. In some dreams, the walls were slowly closing in on me. The dreams seemed to last forever and were reoccurring. When I woke up, I was in constant pain. I had developed pneumonia. During this time, I had nine broken ribs and, sometime later, a total of eleven. Coughing was extremely painful. It started on my back and seemed to vibrate to my chest, especially in my left side and sternum in the middle. I hated to cough, but I was sure it was necessary to remove the harmful mucus or fluid in my lungs.

I remember hearing nurses and doctors describing me in my condition. They said, "All he does is lie there. He seems to be just staring at the ceiling as if he is watching something float across it. He seems to be very boring." I was very scared. What had happened to me? I felt so helpless and couldn't move. I was very, very sick because of my injury. I didn't know if I was going to live or die. If I had died, I knew that I would be going back to heaven in peace and feel God's love without pain.

I was a little confused. My left arm and side were very weak, and I couldn't talk. Maybe I had a stroke? These thoughts went through my mind. For some reason, I tried to talk when nurses came in, but I couldn't speak! I was very scared.

Eventually, as I recovered, I needed a way to communicate with the nurses, doctors, and my family members. I motioned for something to write on as if holding a pen. It often was a difficult task to ask for a clipboard as the nurses couldn't figure out what I wanted. I was handed a clipboard that somebody held while I wrote. I had to figure out how to write without seeing the paper because I couldn't tell the holder I couldn't see it. It often became very frustrating to attempt to communicate with others to let them know my needs. I truly discovered what it must be like for people, especially special-needs children, the difficulties in telling their wants and needs. I had a lot of patience working with children with autism and mentally challenged children and teenagers. I developed a new understanding of the frustrations that people with severe illness and physical or mental challenges face every day of their lives. Mine was only temporary, and it became better through the new challenges I faced in my recovery.

I didn't know that I had a tracheostomy (trach) tube in my throat. Why couldn't I talk? I was finally told that I had a trach by a nurse. A tracheostomy is a surgical procedure to create an opening through the neck into the trachea or windpipe. I was very scared because I thought it would be in my airway for the rest of my life.

I was told that over half of my blood was from transfusion. I am thankful for the people that were blood donors. I remember my brother Michael telling the medical staff that he offered to donate blood to me.

My pains were very intense. The nurses had to clean my helpless body every day. I felt sorry for them, but they were very dedicated to taking care of me. I hated to be rolled to my side to be cleaned and to change the bedding because the pain even made me black out on some occasions. I developed pneumonia and had to have my trach cleaned out from mucus and blood. It was important to keep my breathing and lungs clear from obstructions.

My days sometimes lasted forever that it seemed like there were thirty-six hours in a day. I continued to be hooked up to the machine to help keep my blood flowing properly and using my heart and lungs.

Sometimes, the nurses would drink water in front of me. I had everything intravenously or through my feeding tube, which entered through my nose. I was thinking of how good a single drop of water would taste. Wow! It's really something that I was really missing at the time!

October 17, 2018, was a very difficult day. The respiratory therapist caused me to become very uneasy that day, and I choked and blacked out twice. I finally fell asleep and had a very bad nightmare. I was awake a lot during the night. At 4:00 AM, I seemed to become very nauseated quickly. I vomited a lot on myself and the male nurse. We were talking about my day for the plans to take the ECMO tubes and wires out. The nurse talked to the doctor because there was a concern and problems in my stomach or intestines. A tube that had numbers as a ruler had to be placed in my nostril and pushed down into my stomach to be x-rayed. It was very painful, and it smelled terrible when pushed down. It was almost forty-five minutes before the doctor could read the X-ray. I attempted to not think about being uncomfortable with the tube.

The X-ray was read by the doctor and, after an attempt, failed to push the tube further into my intestines. My eyes were watering because of the pain involved. The results were negative on problems. Little did I know that this would be the beginning of my road to my recovery as I started making positive steps.

The early morning shift changed. I was so lucky to get a very enthusiastic nurse named Brittany! Brittany said, "We are going to have a great day! We are going to have so much fun today!" She started my day with a wonderful mood. That day, I learned how to breathe on my own. I got a change to my trach, and I talked for the first time in a while.

Brittany understood my makeshift sign language when I motioned for her to help. I was very happy that she seemed to read exactly what I thought immediately. She shaved me that day. I asked her if she had ever heard of the New York Jets quarterback Joe Namath and Farrah Fawcett, who was in a Noxzema commercial. She shaved me very carefully because I was on the blood thinner medication Coumadin. Later in the day, I used my phone to show her the commercial on YouTube. I told her she reminded me of Farrah Fawcett.

I had to learn how to breathe again on my own without the assistance of a machine. The air seemed cold on my lungs, but I was motivated by Brittany and myself to try my best to work hard to breathe. It was exhausting work to continue breathing the oxygen through the machine and concentrating on taking as deep breaths as possible for a long period of time. I extended the goal of breathing longer than Brittany had set for me.

I was supposed to meet with the speech therapist to use a talking tube on my trach. I had to learn to do exercises to swallow. It was a necessary step to learn how to drink and eat again. Wow! These are things that we learned as little babies and at a very young age, and I didn't think it would be so complicated! It was important to swallow properly to avoid choking. I tasted my first water on a teaspoon. I had craved this moment for a long time. It was a task that was very important in my recovery process. I had to practice the skills I learned over the weekend in order to pass the eating and drinking test that would be scheduled for early next week.

I craved eating one small strawberry! I wanted to be able to drink water. We take a lot of things that have become second nature for us for granted. I think about the wonderful life that God gave to each of us. God blessed me with another opportunity to praise Him in glory because He gave me the choice to come back to earth from heaven. Somewhere within my body, God was giving me the strength to conquer the obstacles that lay in front of me.

Now it was time to learn how to talk. The speech therapist put a talking trach adapter in its position on the trach. I was to say the letter *A*. I said, "A." Wow! I made the *A* sound! Just like in elementary school! It sounded kind of funny. My sister, Frances, and Brittany were there, and they were very cheerful and happy for me. They said I did well. The speech therapist said to say something else. I said, "Hi, how are you doing?"

I told Brittany about my experience of dying and going to heaven. She was the first nurse whom I told about this beautiful opportunity. Brittany said she had talked to two other patients in the past who had this amazing story of coming back after death. Brittany told me that I should write a book. I told her that I already had planned on writing a book. At the time, I didn't have a title. Brittany went to Catholic school and was very easy to talk to.

I talked to her about me being like Pinocchio with all my strings attached, how I wanted to be free from the strings and, like Pinocchio, live my life unattached. The strings I was talking about were the blood pressure, IVs, feeding tube, and the wires and tubes within my body from the life-support machine.

My brother Michael came in and was happy that I could talk. He called other people in our family and friends for me to talk to. It was enjoyable to let them hear me, yet with all the talking and breathing therapy, I became very tired and worn out.

I had the tubes and wires taken out from the life support, and I started making better improvements. My sister showed the nurse and me a picture of a rainbow that she took that day that appeared to be having one end at my house. I believe that it was a sign from God because I started to become stronger.

I often asked for a damp cloth to put on my forehead as my mom did while I was a child when I had a fever. It seemed to sooth me and to keep me cooler when I was too warm and helped to comfort me.

I was taken out of intensive care to start my road to recovery. I was taken to another area in the hospital to spend the night until I was given another room. I was very hot and didn't sleep very well.

It was Saturday morning at about 4:30 AM when I called to have a priest come to visit me, getting an answering service for Sunday. He called me back within fifteen minutes. I told him that I thought he sounded on the phone to be very young. He said he was thirty-five and that I could talk to an older priest if I wanted to. I told him that his age was perfect and that I would enjoy talking to him. I asked him to bring a Brown Scapular, rosary, and communion for me. I told him that I wanted to tell him about my experience when I died and went to heaven. Later in the day, after talking to the doctor, I was told that I wouldn't be able to take communion until I learned to eat first and swallow. I called the priest, Father Paul, back to tell him. He said that he would look forward to seeing me on Sunday.

I was given another room, and I talked to the nurses and doctors about what happened to me. They were very attentive to me and treated me very nicely. Telling nurses, doctors, respiratory therapists, and physical therapists about falling from my tree stand and how I died and went to heaven became a routine that I really enjoyed.

My body was aching. My feet, legs, and right knee were swollen very badly. I was put on oxygen at night and looked like I either had an octopus or a bagpipe with all the tubes on me. When water in the machine was low or in the air flowing through the tubes, it sounded like drums beating. It kept me awake and was an annoying sound. I would ring for the nurse, and she would fix the problem. Eventually, I called this noise my Little Drummer Boy.

When I would ring for the nurse, I would say, "My Little Drummer Boy is back again!" He likes keeping me awake. The nurses would come in and make the sound stop so I could get back to sleep. I didn't like wearing an oxygen mask at night, but I knew that it was very important for me.

I shared my story with a male nurse who had to change my IV over from my right arm. It was the first time that I spoke about my experience to a man who, although he said he was a Christian, didn't believe my story of dying and going to heaven. I told him that it wasn't up to me the make him believe. I said, "I told you the story of how I died and went to heaven. It's up to you to figure out if you want to believe."

It was difficult for me to talk to this male nurse because he didn't believe my story. I discovered for the first time that it was going to be a challenge to have everyone accept my story. Not all people are going to believe in or have doubts about God's existence, so I had to take this as a learning process. I just accepted the task that God presented to me. My job was to tell people that God and heaven are real. God gave me a gift and an opportunity to come back to earth. I didn't know what my mission was, yet God revealed something to me to present to anyone who would listen. I have become God's humble servant, who is willing even more than ever to talk about the miracle that He has blessed me with.

I was in that room when I got to see the sunrise for the first time since my hospital stay. There were a lot of buildings around the hospital. It was amazing to see the sun rising up into the sky. It was something that I truly missed seeing every day.

I had a physical therapist and her assistant come to my room to help me out of bed and to stand. It was very painful to get out of bed. The therapist had me stand up with assistance. My body was very weak and unbalanced. This was the first time in my life that I really needed to be motivated to stand and try to take my first three steps. My right knee, feet, and legs were very swollen. It was so difficult to take the initial step. The therapist and her assistant helped me and held on to me. I had to trust them to not let me fall as I gave all my strength to move my left leg first. I thought about people who had strokes and accidents and disabled people and veterans who went through this to try to recover. At first, I almost wondered if I would even be able to walk again. I was very nervous and concerned about my right leg and knee because I still didn't know the extent of the damage to it. There was still a blood clot in my leg that made the swelling difficult to reduce. I tried to ice my knee down as much as possible. On my own, I tried to do physical therapy, like leg lifts and bending my knees. I moved my arms, attempting to gain strength in them. My left side in the ribs and my left arm were very weak. It was difficult to get out of bed with the assistance of therapists or nurses. They wanted me to start sitting in a chair. I had to stand and turn to the right to be assisted into the chair. My tailbone hurt a lot when I sit for a long period of time. It took most of my energy to hold my head up. It was very uncomfortable for me to sit, and I became very tired. I was often thankful and relieved when the nurse would let me get back into bed.

It was Sunday, about 10:00 AM. The priest Father Paul came to visit me. I was very happy to have him come and meet with me. He came and talked to me and prayed with me and talked about the Bible. He gave me a Brown Scapular and rosaries. The rosaries touched the rock at Golgotha where Jesus was crucified at the base, and the arm of the cross touched the tomb where Jesus was buried. I tried to insist Father Paul to keep the rosaries, but he insisted that I take them. The rosaries were made in Jerusalem.

I took the rosaries and touched my knee and my ribs with Father Paul present, asking for God to heal my wounds. I told Father Paul that I wanted to speak to people in churches about going to heaven. I told him my story about archery hunting and falling from the tree stand. I told him how I died and went to heaven. He thanked me for telling him about what had happened. He encouraged me to continue getting better, write my book, and pursue my goals. Father Paul gave me another blessing and prayed with me. I thanked him for the gifts that he brought me and for coming to see me.

For the next few days, I joked with the physical therapist and said that it was time for my dancing lessons. I had to learn all over again how to step sideways and forward, then turn around to sit down. It was very exhausting for me and we had to be careful not to get tangled in all the wires and tubes. It was very similar to learning how to dance the waltz. It was fun to make the physical therapists laugh.

I continued talking to nurses, doctors, and physical therapists about my incredible journey to heaven. A respiratory therapist named Aaron came in to take care of me and to clean my trach. When I asked him what his name was, he said it was Aaron. Making a reference to the Bible, I said, "Where's Moses?" I asked him if he believed in God. Aaron told me that he was an atheist. I thought, *Wow! God put him in front of me so I could talk to him.* I asked Aaron if I could tell him my story about going to heaven. He said that I could. Aaron listened very intently to me.

He did a great job clearing my trach and explained what I needed to do to relax and made me feel more at ease. I thanked him for treating me so well and told him that he was a very nice man. I was very pleased with the help that he did for me.

I really liked the nurses, doctors, and complete medical staff who helped me. They really listened to my needs, concerns, and suggestions to help turn me to clean either me or my bedding for me.

I had a nurse named Felicia who worked with me one night. She was a very good nurse. During one of her visits during the night, she brought fresh ice water in for me. She was moving some machines, not realizing that the feeding tube in my nose and other wires were attached without very much slack. I was holding the ice water with my right hand, and suddenly, the feeding tube became tighter. The feeding tube was pulling on my nose and hurting my nostrils. I was like a fish on a hook and line being caught by a fisherman. I was almost pulled out of my bed. I yelled, "Whoa! Stop!" Felicia stopped, immediately realizing what had happened.

Felicia left the room a short time later. About twenty minutes had elapsed since she left. I had been coughing and having a difficult time breathing. It seemed like something was stuck in my windpipe. I used the buzzer to call the nurse back into the room. She had the respiratory therapist Aaron come back in to attempt to clear my trach.

I was coughing continuously while having dizziness. My eyes were watering, and my chest was hurting because of the coughing. I had to keep my composure because I was becoming worried. I wasn't sure if it was going to become an emergency situation. I didn't want that. I have encountered too many scary problems as I desperately tried to breathe and tried not to panic.

Felicia and another nurse were watching me, trying to diagnose what was happening to me. Aaron was trying to clear my trach with no success. The other nurse was watching the feeding tube as I coughed. She noticed that the feeding tube was moving in and out of my noise almost half an inch at a time. I had suspected that the feeding tube had been bothering me ever since I got sick a few days ago. I knew that I was hoping that it would be removed.

Felicia called the doctor on staff to find out what to do. Although it took a while, the doctor gave her the permission to remove the feeding tube. After she carefully and slowly removed the tube, I coughed a little more. Aaron again worked to clear my trach. About five minutes later, I started to feel much better. I was breathing better and stopped coughing. I was very relieved! I thanked the nurses and Aaron, telling them that I felt as if they saved my life. I later joked with them and other doctors and nurses that Felicia took me on a fishing trip. I said, "Wow! How exciting! During the month of October, I went to heaven, had two helicopter rides, and went on a fishing trip!"

I believe it was God's plan to speed up my recovery. I was previously scheduled to learn how to eat and swallow food on my own. I had to be able to pass the eating test. I was very nervous and determined to pass the test. I said many prayers asking God to help me pass the eating test. I was very worried about taking the test and didn't have a lot of confidence in myself. I was determined that I would leave it in God's hands.

On Monday, I was scheduled to have my eating test done. I was very nervous for the test because I wanted it to be successful. If I weren't able to eat and swallow, I feared that the medical staff would put another feeding tube in my nose. I prayed to God numerous times early in the morning. The speech therapist came to get me and take me to the testing area where a special dye was put into a yogurt to eat. The dye was used so that the food could be tracked as it went down my esophagus into my stomach by using an X-ray. It was difficult for me to sit up for a long period of time in the chair.

My upper body was very weak. The strength to keep my head up was a challenge for me. The yogurt wasn't very tasty, but I knew that it was important to be able to swallow it successfully. I had practiced my swallowing skills since last week. I didn't know that retraining to eat would be such a challenging task. I said many prayers during the night and morning before my eating test. I was very nervous and wanted to pass the eating test so I would be able to eat on my own.

I was given other things with more texture to eat. I had to eat and drink water to aid in flushing the food down my esophagus. Then I had small cookie chunks mixed into the yogurt. Wow! I thought of cookies and cream ice cream. It was a little more difficult to swallow as I washed it down with water. I passed my test! Hooray! I was very excited. I would be able to eat my first meal soon. I said a prayer and thanked God for helping through the test and for passing.

I went back to my room to have my first meal. My friends Jim Hickernell and Kevin Pipp, whom I knew from the Meadville YMCA, came to visit me. The physical and occupational therapist showed up at the same time as my first meal was delivered. The two therapists said that I had to get up and walk before I could eat. My friends Jim and Kevin had to go to the waiting room for a few minutes. I teased the therapists and told them about denying me of my first meal. I told them that I might starve to death because they wanted me to do therapy first before eating.

I had to stand up and march in place. It was so difficult to march, picking my knees up carefully ten times. I still didn't have very good balance yet and needed to be assisted to stand and be supported so I wouldn't fall.

The therapist reheated my food for me. It was important for me to remember the steps for eating. First, take a bite and chew and swallow and then drink. Eat, then drink each time I took a bite to make sure it went down the esophagus.

My friends Jim and Kevin came back in the room. They got to watch me eat my first meal since I first entered the hospital in early October. The meal was steak sliced up into very tiny chunks and potatoes with gravy and beans. I had mandarin oranges. The food actually tasted pretty good. Jim and Kevin visited with me while I took each bite with small scoops on my spoon. I drank from a cup of ice water to help wash the food down. I found out that my stomach must have shrunk because I had a difficult time eating all my food.

Jim teased me and said that it wasn't hard to learn how to eat. He and Kevin showed me a video on the phone from a couple of my YMCA friends near my favorite exercise bike. They were wishing me to get well soon. Jim bought a Pittsburgh Pirates hat for me and gave it to me as a gift. I put it on, and we made a video to send back for the YMCA members to see. It was very nice to have my friends visit from Meadville and coming down to the hospital at UPMC Presbyterian. We had a really fun time talking, and I felt the support and prayers from all the YMCA members.

I was very happy to see my friends Jim and Kevin. I had talked to them both on the phone. It was really nice to have them visit and talk to me about the friends whom I missed from the gym. It was nice that they came down and teased me, making my first meal pleasant.

I continued telling my story about dying to nurses and doctors. I had a male nurse come in, and as I told him about seeing the most handsome man I ever saw, he said, "That's because you hadn't met me yet!" We both laughed. I said, "Well, I guess you're right!" We continued laughing. I told him that he shouldn't make me laugh because it hurt my ribs.

I had a nurse whom I had never met before come in to give me medication one night close to midnight.

She said, "You look very beautiful!"

I said, "Really? I never thought of myself as looking beautiful."

She said, "Yes, you are very beautiful!"

I replied, "Well, I guess that's possible because I died and went to heaven. I haven't looked in a mirror lately." Joking, I reached up and touched my bald head and asked, "Do I have my hair back?" We both laughed.

My nurses who took care of me were wonderful, dedicated, and very caring people. It was a challenge for me to get out of bed and move even with their assistance. From each nurse, I learned something helpful to make life in the hospital easier. I had problems sleeping at night. I became constipated and didn't have bowel movements consistently because of the medication I was on. When I would finally use the bed pan, it seemed that the pain of constipation would come back and bother me about three to four hours later.

I used a catheter to urinate, and I drank a lot of water. Eventually, I was taken off catheter, and my body had to adjust to using urinal in bed. I found it much easier when I could have a nurse help me sit up at the side of the bed. Sometimes, it was difficult to get started because my body needed to learn how to react again.

Nurses Liz and Hannah often came in and saw that I was not sleeping during the night. I enjoyed talking to them and making them laugh. They tried to encourage me to do as much as I could by myself. They came in and told me that if they caught me on my phone one more time, they would take it away. I watched YouTube songs or videos to make my sleepless nights more enjoyable. I was watching a comedy show when Liz walked in again. She asked me what I was doing on my phone. I told her I was running out of things to say to make her laugh. She took my phone as I surrendered it and put it on the other side of the table beside me where I couldn't reach it. Liz and Hannah told me that I could have it back if I slept for a while. They teased me and said they would probably hear me falling out of bed trying to get my phone back. I assured them that *that* wouldn't happen. We all laughed, but I went to sleep. Liz kept her promise and gave my phone back to me before morning.

My routine changed, and I had to spend time sitting in a chair. My upper body was very weak, and I struggled to sit for a long period of time. My head seemed to be heavy, and my neck became tired when trying to support it. My tailbone was sore, and I became very uncomfortable when sitting a long time. The doctors said that my tailbone was probably sore because of the fall.

The nurses and doctors encouraged me to do as much as I could on my own. One night, my remote for the television and call button fell on the floor. I had no way to call the nurses if I needed help. I used my arm to push the table out of the way and used my left leg to lift the cord of the remote off the floor until I could reach it with my hands. The nurse was proud of me. I used my intelligence and moved my leg to overcome the difficult task of picking up the remote.

One morning, a doctor came in to check on me. He told me that I had developed quite a reputation.

I said, "What do you mean?"

He said, "You've been telling everybody the story of how you died and went to heaven."

I asked, "Do you want to hear it?"

He said, "No, I have already heard about it."

I asked, "Do you want me to stop telling it?"

He said, "No, keep telling it."

I said, "Thank you. I will."

Every day, I started doing more exercises on my own to strengthen my muscles. I did leg lifts and bent my knees as much as possible. I did movements with my arms for flexibility and strength. It was necessary that I get stronger to lift myself out of bed. The nurses and therapists would crank up the top part of my bed where my head rested. It was very difficult to lie flat on the bed. The bed was at an incline and always seemed to act like a sliding board. I would often slide down toward the bottom of the bed. It would become very uncomfortable to lie down. The nurses would flatten out my bed, and they would work together on each side of me to pull me up toward the top again. They had me hold on to a pillow or pull my arms to my chest so my ribs wouldn't hurt as bad. I would tell the nurses that they were pulling me up the sliding board so I could ride down again.

I was supposed to go see the Pittsburgh Steelers and the Cleveland Browns play on October 28, 2018, with my friend Jim Zill. I had purchased the tickets in the month of August through the Slippery Rock University alumni. I was really looking forward to going to the game with him. Unfortunately, I had my accident falling from the tree stand. Since I wasn't going to be able to go to the game, I had a goal to get more yards than Le'Veon Bell in Pittsburgh since I was the only one in the city, and he wasn't. I had walked about 30 yards earlier in the week. The day before the game, I walked 60 yards. I told the doctors, nurses, and physical therapists that I wanted all my visits and therapy before kickoff time. My goal was to walk one hundred yards to gain more yards than Bell on Sunday. When

Sunday morning came, I walked 113 yards. It was difficult, and I was very tired when I finished, but I made it to my goal.

My brother Michael and Jim went to the game where it was cold and raining. I guess for the day, I had the best possible seat in the hospital where I was warm and dry. Michael and Jim came to visit me after the game. Michael bought a Halloween Terrible Towel for me. It was nice to have them visit after the game to tell me about their experience. They showed me pictures that they took at the game.

On Monday, I had to walk over a hundred yards in the morning for a cardiologist. Later in the day, the physical therapist came in, and I had to do over one hundred more yards.

Tuesday came, and I once again had two different sessions to walk over one hundred yards. I joked that I was going to have more yards than Le'Veon Bell. I was disappointed that he didn't sign with Pittsburgh Steelers yet this season. I was very excited about James Conner becoming a Pittsburgh Steelers running back. He went to McDowell High School in Erie, Pennsylvania, and I followed his career. He went to the Pittsburgh Panthers and was having a great career until he hurt his knee and was later diagnosed with Hodgkin's disease. He is a good role model for perseverance. I was glad that the Steelers drafted him.

I was making good progress, and the doctors, nurses, and physical therapists were encouraging me. My body was still very weak. I was supposed to sit in a chair for as long as possible. My butt near the tailbone was very sore to sit on for a prolonged period of time. I knew it was an important part of my rehabilitation to sit and strengthen my core muscles while letting my heart work to pump blood throughout my body. I used my time sitting to watch a Christian broadcast station and eat my breakfast, lunch, or supper. I watched more college football than I ever have, and I was definitely watching more Christian programs.

I got permission to use the bathroom on my own for the first time while the nurse stayed outside of the door. I was slowly making progress. The medical staff encouraged me by saying that I improved a lot that week.

Wednesday was going to be my last day at UPMC Presbyterian. I got out of bed to use the bathroom, and the alarm went off in my room. Two nurses came to my bathroom door, knocking to see if I was okay. I said that I was. The alarm was on my bed, and when the weight of my body was off, it started ringing. After I finished using the bathroom, I asked the nurses if they ran down the hall to my room because they got there very fast. They said they did run because they were worried about me. I joked with the nurses that since it was my last day at UPMC Presbyterian, I was planning my escape. I told them that I guess they caught me. I surrender!

On October 31, 2018, I had to wash myself with a washcloth. I had to stand in the bathroom and prepare everything myself with soap and towels for drying. Since I was standing so long, my heart was racing very fast. I told the nurse I had to sit down. She told me that I would have to finish washing first. I was very worried because my heart was pounding so hard that I was afraid that I could have a heart attack. Washing my body then was harder than any exercise workout program I had ever done in my life. When I was finally able to lie down, it took a long time to recover as my heart continued to beat rapidly. I was relieved when my heart slowed down.

I had my last day of physical therapy. I told the doctors and nurses that they did a very good job of taking care of me and thanked them for the good job that they did. I told the nurses to let everyone who worked with me know that they were great people and that I appreciated all that they did for me while I was in the hospital.

I had my trach removed in my room. I was a little scared about having it taken out because I did not know what to expect. I thought that it might be a long procedure and didn't know that I would be awake while it happened. The trach was removed. I only experienced a little bit of pain while it was being completed. I was told to cover up the trach when I talked and coughed for at least five to seven days. It had to have time to heal properly.

In the days past, my brother Michael wanted to have me go to physical therapy in Andover, Ohio. I told my sister, Frances, and she found out that I could go to HealthSouth in Erie, Pennsylvania. My brother Michael was retired from teaching, and it was closer to him at Andover. My sister said that Erie would be closer and more convenient for her daughter Amy and her to come see me. It was arranged that I was to be transferred to HealthSouth for physical therapy.

I took a ride in an ambulance to HealthSouth later in the day. It was a cold day to ride in an ambulance. I was used to being in the hospital where temperatures were anywhere from seventy-five to close to ninety degrees during my stay. The ride was at times uncomfortable on my butt and back, so I repositioned my body several times during the two and a half hour ride. I enjoyed talking to the emergency medical technician on the way to HealthSouth. I told her my story about dying and going to heaven. She told me that she had a sister who died in a car wreck. It was sad to hear her tell about it. She believed in God and knew her sister was in heaven. Talking to her made the ride go much quicker.

I was nervous about going to rehabilitation. During my stay at UPMC Presbyterian, my sister kept asking me to find out how long it might take to get out of rehabilitation physical therapy. I asked the doctor who evaluated me and gave me a diagnosis how long it might take. He tested me for strength in my legs and arms and range of motion. He told me that usually it takes three to four weeks. My niece Amy wanted to invite me for Thanksgiving that year. I had to set a personal goal to work hard and get out before Thanksgiving.

I was told that physical therapy would be very difficult and challenging because I would be scheduled for about four hours a day. At HealthSouth, the nurses demanded that I did as much as I could on my own. Dr. James was a respiratory therapist. He came in and examined my trach. He said that the doctors at UPMC Presbyterian did a wonderful job. He said that it was one of the top 15 percent that he ever saw done. He told me that it would probably only leave very little scar. He just put a Band-Aid on it for a couple days. It was one of my concerns—I believed I would have a bad scar for the rest of my life on my throat. I made sure to call UPMC Presbyterian to tell them that the doctor said they did a great job on my trach. I wasn't able to see it yet, and it was very good news for me to hear that the scar would be hardly noticeable.

My first night was very restless. I had been watching a lot of Christian broadcast stations while I was at UPMC Presbyterian. I spent the night watching some religious programs at HealthSouth. The change in my environment and the new bed and demands of not knowing what to expect for the first day of physical therapy kept me awake during the night. It was difficult adjusting my schedule to getting medication during the different times of the night. I had an infection in my right groin from the ECMO where the staples were near my femoral artery. I was very concerned about the infection. I was worried because when the staples used as stitches were removed at UPMC Presbyterian, it was opening up. The staples had to stay in my leg until the wound healed. Often I feared the worst, that my leg would be amputated! I was put on antibiotics to help fight the infection. It was very sore and warm in this part of my leg.

Taking my medication by mouth was difficult. I had to have the pills broken into small pieces and taken with applesauce or pudding. I would get the pills stuck in my throat and need water to wash them down. It was a very scary feeling to have a pill get stuck in my throat. Sometimes, I would run out of water trying to help the pill down my throat, and the nurse would have to hurry to get me more water.

That night, when I had to use the bathroom, instead of calling for the nurse, I slowly got out of bed and went in the bathroom, and the alarm went off. When the nurse arrived, I said I was trying to escape. I told the nurse I thought I had permission to get out of bed. I did have permission, but the nurse preferred to be there for me.

My first day of physical therapy arrived. I was taken down the physical therapy room in a wheelchair. I had to do exercises with the wheelchair using my arms and legs to move myself around the room. I had experienced riding in a wheelchair at a summer camp where I worked for the first time in 1985. I remembered that it was a challenge to use my arms as I used it. I did well maneuvering the wheelchair around the beds that were used for therapy.

I had to do leg exercises to strengthen my legs, like leg extensions, raises, and marching while seated. I learned how to walk up and down stairs safely. While doing the exercises, I had a heating pad on the left side of my sore ribs.

I had speech therapy with a therapist named Diane. She was testing my memory and thinking skills. The first words she wanted me to remember were *bed*, *blue*, and *socks*. She told me that she would ask it to me a little later in our testing session. I asked Diane when her birthday was. She told me it was November 9th. I knew it would be easy to remember since it was eight days away. I didn't tell her, but one of my gifts was that I could remember birthdays, names, and before we had cell phones, phone numbers. She asked me many questions, and I gave her correct answers on all but one. I guess I thought of the answer too quickly and was incorrect. She asked, "What is on top, your head or your neck?" I answered too quickly without thinking, saying my neck.

Diane asked all the questions and said we were running out of time. She asked, "What were the three words I wanted you to remember?" I said, "Oh no! I knew you were going to ask me those words. Okay, let me try. Diane went to bed on November 9th with blue socks on!" I think I surprised her with remembering all those things and using them in one sentence.

Melissa, the first therapist I had for the day, asked me, "Based on today, what are your goals?" The first thing I said was, "I want to be out of physical therapy in a week!" Then I added, "I want to work with the therapist with cooperation and learn everything I can to make that possible."

The therapist surprised me. I was in the physical therapy room and was given instructions to take the wheelchair back to my room. I was asked if I remembered my room number. I was told directions on how to get back to my room. I was told how to get out of the wheelchair safely by locking the wheels and then getting into bed.

I started down the hallway and was going very slow. I joked with a nurse walking down the hall saying they left me off at the physical therapy room thirty-two miles away from my room without a wheelchair license and expected me to find my way without a map. Wow! It seemed such a long way from the room. It was a very demanding exercise for me to accomplish. I was getting very tired using my arm and leg muscles. I saw that my room number was getting closer. I had the incentive to keep going. I didn't want to fail the task the physical therapist gave me. As I arrived in my room, I felt a sense of accomplishment. When I went back to the room, I laid in my bed and cried. God had given me the strength for all the people praying for me. I was surprised how well I did for the first day of physical therapy.

I ended the night by getting instructions to take a shower and wash myself. I was to sit under the shower in a chair with washcloths. I shaved myself by sitting in a chair before I took the shower. It really felt good to take a shower although it was very tiring and challenging. I didn't know that shaving and taking a shower were so much work.

Once again, it was difficult to sleep. My pain level was still very high. I often said to the nurses and doctors that based on the scale of 1 to 10, 10 being the worst, it was about 11 or 12. Today, it was 10 or 11 for the pain level. It was very hard to sleep because I was warm. I also had a difficult time swallowing the pill again. I needed a lot of water to get the pill down.

Everything about my rehabilitation was about trying to be able to do things for myself. With my limited strength, flexibility, and balance, changing clothes was a very difficult task. Putting my shirt on was the easiest. It was difficult to put my underwear, sweatpants, socks, and shoes on. I had to have a nurse help me put on my shoes and tie them for me.

When I woke up for the second day of rehabilitation, I believe that God granted me a wonderful miracle. The pain in my ribs on my left side had a pain level I usually described as 11 or 12. On this morning, I woke up with a pain level of 3 or 4. My left side felt so much better overnight. I thanked God and said a prayer for this great miracle that He had given me.

It was a great day for my physical therapy because I started to lift weights. I started out lifting one pound in each arm. I told the physical therapist, "I don't want to brag, but I can lift one pound!" I had to do three sets of ten repetitions with a big rest in between.

I also had to look at pictures and sort them out in a safe or unsafe pile. The therapist was very firm about doing things safe in my very fragile condition so I wouldn't fall or have an accident.

I continued speech therapy, which was more of a challenge. I had to use my math skills and be able to add, subtract, multiply, and divide. I had to be able to give change counting backward like we did before computers were used to do it. I had to use real money to give back the correct change. I know that it was difficult for me to really be mentally focused, and I felt some testing pressure and anxiety to be careful to get the problems correct. I wanted to be perfect. When I was confused about a problem, I asked the speech therapist, Diane, for a pencil and paper in order to write the problem down. I used this method for writing down the numbers and then was more comfortable giving the correct change when the problems became more difficult.

I had to walk on a floor with a different texture of a mat and gravel, making sure to walk carefully and not to go too fast. It was like walking on a very rough, uneven terrain. It was a physical challenge for me that I felt my leg muscles working to keep my balance.

I was in the physical therapy room looking around at people who were patients. I saw people with one arm, one leg or no legs, and many who had physical handicaps. I looked around and saw the people whom God wanted me to talk to. I thought of all the miracles God performed on people who were sick, blind, or lame. I looked down at my body. I still had my legs, my feet, my toes, my arms, my hands, and all my fingers. I had my eyes, and I could see. I had my ears, and I could hear. I silently thanked God for all that He had given me. I was slowly getting better, stronger, and physically and mentally stronger each and every day! I said, "God, You put me with these people in front of me for a reason. You wanted me to appreciate what You have given to me. I will do my best to talk to them, to tell my story, and tell them that heaven and You are real!" I had tears in my eyes as I looked at the people around me. It really touched my heart to see the physical therapists working with them with the patience and the desire to help them.

The therapists let me tell the other patients my story of dying and going to heaven. I enjoyed talking to them about their life and got to know each patient. A few times, the physical therapists brought patients to me to have me talk to them and encourage them to work hard in physical therapy to get stronger.

I was very happy to share my story with anyone! God gave me a special gift and opportunity that I was using to tell people about God's love for us. The patients were very receptive and were encouraged not only by my story but also that I took the time to hear about them. I was truly grateful to God for giving me the opportunity to touch the lives of people in the hospital.

After therapy, I was to use the wheelchair again to travel to my room. At least this time I knew how to get there without directions. It still seemed far to use my arms and feet to wheel myself to my room.

Prior to my third day of physical therapy, I had Dr. Dave come into my room to check on my condition. I told him my story and told him that I was planning on writing a book about it. He told me that he works with people every day who had cancer and were dying. He told me that my story would be very motivational and inspiring for them to hear. He told me that when I get my book written and published, he would like me to bring him a copy of it up to the HealthSouth Hospital for him. I told him that I would try my best to make sure that he gets a copy.

On my third day of physical therapy, I was told that there was a physical therapist intern from my hometown of Saegertown, Pennsylvania, who would be working with me that day. As it turned out, it was somebody whom I hadn't seen for a long time. It was a girl whom I knew when she was still in high school named Sadie Brunot. I didn't recognize her at first because she was still in her early teens when I saw her last time. I was a substitute teacher in her school. I asked her what her last name was, and she said Brunot. I said, "Oh yes, you are Sadie!" I knew her mom and dad, grandmother and grandfather, and her uncle John, who I played high school football with. I was very excited about having Sadie as one of my physical therapists that day. She did a great job working with me and was a very caring person. I watched her work with other patients. She truly was going to become a good physical therapist. Later in the evening,

I called her grandparents Bob and Louise Brunot to tell them that their granddaughter was my physical therapist for the day.

Physical therapy got more demanding every day. I was discovering more things that I was able to do physically and mentally. Speech therapy was still a challenge for me. I needed to concentrate and keep my focus. I learned to be careful and think about the correct answers.

I was able to talk to more nurses and patients. Each day, I seemed to draw a crowd of two or three patients who had time to talk to me. I also got to meet another man who fell from his tree stand and broke his leg. We talked about bowhunting deer and hunting turkeys. He talked about the importance and safety of using a safety harness at all times going up, down, and up again in the stand and always checking your tree stands before the season. As I write this book, I want the hunters who read it to be safe and enjoy the hunt. I was lucky to be alive from my accident. Even if you don't hunt, it's important to always think about your safety to avoid an accident.

Over the next few days of my physical therapy, I got to meet a cleaning lady who had a near-death experience. She said that her husband came home drunk and was yelling at her. He didn't want to give her the keys to the car. He started the car and ran her over. She said that she went into the house and believed she was dying. While lying on the couch, she felt God's presence. She said that she was healed.

The next day, the physical therapist told me that they wanted to introduce me to somebody else who had a story similar to mine. I was introduced to a man. He said, "You can call me Mr. Williams." Mr. Williams had one leg amputated because he started doing drugs. He developed kidney problems and had to go on kidney dialysis.

He told me about his experience, how God forgave him and gave him a chance to continue living. Mr. Williams said that he had a great father. His mother and father got a divorce. His dad did everything with him and suddenly stopped doing anything with him. He started doing drugs and selling them as a teenager. He eventually developed kidney problems and died. He was given a chance to live. You could tell by talking with Mr. Williams that his experience really changed his life. He had a deep devotion to God.

Today, I heard some pretty good news. I had mentioned to the physical therapist Don that I was related to two physical therapists. He came back to me later in the day and told me that I might be able to go home soon if I could follow up in physical therapy with Ryan.

I continued speech and physical therapy. In speech therapy, I had a difficult task of naming streets from clues given in a sentence. Some of the streets were named, and I had to read the clues in the sentences to come up with the street names. I had to label the map. For me, it was difficult to focus on this task. I learned to cross out the clues as I finished the streets and labeled them. I made some mistakes, but the speech therapist worked with me to make the necessary corrections. This activity definitely challenged my thinking skills.

Physical therapy was always demanding for me to learn ways to make the tasks of getting into and out of bed, into and out of a car, walking on loose gravel, taking a shower, and getting dressed easier. I was still having a difficult time with my upper body and my core strength. I had to stay attentive on walking to keep my balance and to go around obstacles within the physical therapy room. I was becoming more confident in my walking as I went further. I would still get very tired from walking only a short distance, which seemed like walking for miles. I needed a lot of rest in between workout sessions of walking, riding a recumbent bike, and weight lifting. I was also supposed to use the wheelchair to travel back to my room after the morning and afternoon therapy sessions. Although it was very demanding, I could tell I was getting stronger and in better physical condition.

The best part of my day was to be able to talk to other patients about falling from my tree stand and talking about dying and going to heaven. Physical therapists would keep bringing the patients to me to talk because they wanted to hear my story. I was always happy to talk to them. I was very proud and confident to talk about God and how He gave me the opportunity to continue living.

As I received more daily sessions of physical therapy, it became easier for me to get up and use the bathroom. I had to use nonslipping socks to be careful not to fall in the bathroom. Every day, I was worried about becoming off-balanced or slipping and falling. I wasn't able to bend forward to watch where my feet were going. I had to watch ahead to check for obstacles that might be in the way.

I got the good news that I would be released from physical therapy from HealthSouth. It seemed like the day would never come. I was going to live with my sister, Frances, and my brother-in-law Bob. My brother Michael would be picking me up. I kept looking at the clock and couldn't sleep. I wanted to be out of the hospital so much.

On my first day back home from the hospital, I arranged with my good lawyer friend Alan Pepecilli's secretaries to come visit him after his noon workout at the YMCA to surprise him. I wanted to get a haircut and shave, so I went to the barbershop first. Alan's birthday is on June 11, the same day as one of his heroes Vince Lombardi, whom we both consider to be one of the best coaches in the National Football League. I would often go to his office with a birthday card signed by Vince Lombardi and a quote for his birthday. During my stay at HealthSouth, I recorded Vince Lombardi on YouTube to play for him when I came home from the hospital. I went to his office and waited outside in my truck to watch him go into the office before I entered. My phone battery had drained, so I desperately used my charger in the truck to have enough battery life to play the recording for him. When I greeted him, I told Al that I brought someone back from heaven to talk to him. I jokingly told him that it was my proof that I had died and went to heaven. I played the Vince Lombardi quote for him, and he enjoyed it very much. He asked the secretaries to take a picture of us. Later, I asked my friend Kevin Pipp, who is a graphic designer, to make a picture of Al, Vince Lombardi, the trombone player whom I accidently ran over when I played high school football, and me to give to him as a Christmas present.

Living with my sister and brother-in-law became a challenge, especially in adjusting my new schedule to theirs. I was responsible for doing the dishes, keeping my room clean, cleaning the kitchen, and doing the laundry. I cooked my own breakfast and lunch, then Bob would make supper.

It was difficult for me to walk in the house and up and down the stairs to the basement to do the laundry. I could only go short distances and needed to sit down. Standing in one place for only a few minutes made my heart rate go up rapidly, and it exhausted me. My heart and body were not used to the challenge of standing because I had been lying in the hospital for so long. I could only carry a couple pieces of clothing up and down the stairs at the same time. I had to concentrate on keeping my balance and did one stair at a time as I had learned in physical therapy. I had to be careful not to trip and fall. My left leg was the strongest because of the bruise on my right knee and still had soreness and swelling. I picked the left leg up to climb stairs first, followed by the right leg to the same stair. Going down the stairs was the opposite. I led with my right leg to go down the stairs and followed with the left leg doing one step at a time. Unlike when I had physical therapy, there wasn't a side rail to hold on to while I climbed up or down the stairs. I was very scared to go up and down the stairs because nobody would be home if I fell.

After I went down the basement and came back upstairs, I would have to rest for a long period of time. I began to realize again what it might be like to be recovering from a heart attack, stroke, or many other physical challenges that people face every day. I appreciated the military veterans and people injured in accidents where they lost an arm, leg, or more than one body part. I understood more about the challenges that an accident or illness can place on an individual.

I remember a student asking me a question while I was substitute-teaching after I first got out of college. There was a student in the gym that was graduating from high school who had a severe physical handicap and could not walk or talk. She said, "Why does God let people like him be born like that?" It was a very difficult question for me to answer. I responded, "God wanted us to appreciate what He gave to us."

I think about how lucky I was to fall from the tree stand and only break five ribs and bruise my knee. I eventually had eleven broken ribs. I fell backward headfirst and could have landed on my head, breaking my neck, my back, my arms, or my legs. I could have died or been crippled for life from my accident. I give my praise to God for the challenges that He presented to me. I believe that God wanted me to survive the fall, to be hurt bad enough to die, to be challenged by the injuries where I had to learn how to talk, walk, eat, and drink all over again. God blessed me with an opportunity to give glory to Him and share my story with others. I have become His humble servant to help people become encouraged and to seek hope in God's promises to us as our savior. God gave me the opportunity to see heaven! It was a very beautiful and tranquil place. I felt peace and love enter my soul. I could see forever! I felt very welcomed there by God's love.

I believe that God wanted me to come back to earth. He read my mind and gave me a choice! When he asked me if I wanted to come back to earth, I said, "Yes." Jesus raised Lazarus, a girl, and a boy from the dead. He cured the lame, the blind, and the sick! I believe that God performed another miracle!

It was very cold when I got out the hospital. I went to work out at the Meadville YMCA every morning. I had to continue riding the recumbent bike since I started it at HealthSouth. I always joked about the bike, calling it Grandpa's Bike. It was necessary to ride the recumbent bike because my chest, abdomen, and arms didn't have strength. I wanted to develop my legs so I would be able to walk and get more balance and stamina.

Every morning, I would ride the recumbent bike for two sessions. I kept track of my level, time, speed, and distance in a notebook. I wanted to see improvement, and at first, it was very slow. My friend Kevin Pipp helped to motivate me like a trainer. He supported me and encouraged me when I made progress. My friends and many new people whom I met during the return to the YMCA would take time to talk to me. I was always happy to speak to as many people about my experience in heaven. I would listen to Christian music out loud on my phone. People didn't complain about me playing the music without headphones.

I started out doing two sessions for ten minutes. I would rest for about five minutes before I would continue the next session. I was inspired by people and friends to tell my story about heaven.

I would go home to my sister's house and take a shower. The floor in the locker room and shower area at the gym were very slippery. I didn't have good balance and had to be careful not to fall because my ribs were continuing to heal. If I fell down, I would need someone to help me up. I know that I couldn't get up off the floor or ground and often was nervous about falling. I worried when there were snow and ice outside. I slipped many times without falling. I thanked God that I didn't fall. It would have been very dangerous for me, and I didn't want to go back to the hospital.

I went to church for the first time since I was out of the hospital. I went into the church social center, and many people gathered around to welcome me. They wanted to hear my story about how I died and went to heaven. Our church is a small church with usually fifty people or less in church on Sunday. About fifteen people gathered around to listen to me talk about my experience before mass. I enjoyed telling them as they listened to me talk. I thanked them for praying for me. I wanted to have the opportunity to thank them at the end of church. I got an inspiration to thank them at the end of the mass. I asked Father Mark Nowak permission to talk when things were quiet, although later after mass, he told me to ask for permission to talk prior to mass because he didn't like to change plans.

I slowly walked up to the podium in front of the church. I said, "I wanted to thank everybody for praying for me! Your prayers and my faith and love for God saved me!" I was in tears as I talked to the church members. I appreciated my friends at church who prayed for me to recover. I was only able to sit in church and stand very briefly because I wasn't strong enough yet. I wasn't able to kneel down in church because my right knee was still very sore and my core strength was weak.

I went to Vernon Place, which was part of the Meadville Medical Center in Pennsylvania. I went to hand in my prescription for twelve sessions of physical therapy. My physical therapist was my niece Amy's husband, Ryan. I knew most of the physical therapists working there because I was a coach and substitute teacher. It would still be almost three weeks before I would attend my first session. I needed to continue the training that I learned from HealthSouth Hospital on my own for a while.

During my workout every other day, I had to lift weights for my upper body. One day when I started out, Jeff Bradshaw, who I played high school football with, said, "Why don't you lift ten pounds?"

He didn't know how weak I was. When I was lifting weights with the group of men at the YMCA prior to my injury, we always teased each other in a fun way. Alan Pepicelli, my good lawyer friend, often teased Jeff and almost anybody. I said, "I don't want to show off to Al and make him look bad!" We all laughed at my joke.

It was a physical and mental challenge to walk down the stairs to the basement where the weight room was. I was excited by the greetings and encouragement from the friends who supported me and helped motivate me to work hard to get stronger.

I parked every day across the street from the YMCA. It was difficult to walk across the street and avoid the ice and snow. I was very nervous about falling on the icy sidewalk. Some kind friends from the YMCA would help me out by holding my hand and arm to support me while walking. I thanked them for their help and patience with me.

Each day, I got stronger by working hard on my self-rehabilitation. I went to Slippery Rock University for health and physical education and coached football, basketball, volleyball, and softball. I knew that it was important to train for myself. I set goals to get faster and increase the level on the recumbent bike. I would ride two sessions on the bike followed by weight lifting every other day. I would rest between bike riding sessions for five to six minutes. I would make sure that I drank water and tried to recover, then begin the next bike riding session.

Weight lifting was a very slow process to see my improvement. My left side by my ribs was extremely tender and sore. I could barely lift one pound.

I enjoyed sharing my story about dying and going to heaven with new people every day. I jokingly told people that God was a Pittsburgh Steelers fan because the Steelers were undefeated 8–0 while I was in the hospital. As it turned out, they started losing games after I returned home and missed the playoffs. My friends told me that I should have stayed in the hospital until after the Super Bowl! I enjoyed telling people about my near-death experience. It was my way of giving praise and thanks to God for the miracle He had given me.

Every day became another opportunity to spread my story about God and heaven. I enjoyed meeting new people with a new confidence to give them the chance to strengthen their faith as I revealed the gift of continued life that God gave to me. As I experienced my new life that God presented to me, people also inspired me to work out harder to gain my strength and endurance.

When people talked to me, they would say that my job's not done yet. God wanted me to continue on with life so that I could present my experience to them. My friends Cindy and John Weber gave me the opportunity to share my story with them. I asked them to ask their priest if I could talk to him. I asked a priest named Father Dan Hoffman if I could speak to him about possibly sharing my story with his church, Our Lady of the Lake in Edinboro, Pennsylvania. On November 14, 2018, just a little over a month since I died and went to heaven, I went to meet him. I believe that God wants me to speak to people in church and also to write a book. Father Dan told me that I was a saint. I told him that I was just God's humble servant and that I wanted to share the story with the people in his church. When my mom was alive, we would go to church on Saturday night sometimes. She really liked the priest, and it was a very beautiful church. The Our Lady of the Lake Church was funded and built thanks to a thrift store within the old church. I suddenly had a strong desire to speak in churches about the gift that God had given to me. It wasn't something I felt immediately after my accident. I got the desire because of my miraculous recovery that God presented to me.

I continued exercising and speaking about God and my recovery every day. I was slowly making progress with walking. I had a chance to speak in front of the people at St. Philip Church in Linesville, Pennsylvania. I went to church an hour early to ask Father Chris permission to talk and thank the people for praying for me. I was put on the church prayer list by a friend. I sat in the back of the church, and he called me up at the end of mass. It took a while to walk to the front of the church to the podium. During Father Chris's sermon, I reflected on my life as he spoke. He seemed to be talking about me. Father Chris talked about how God, heaven, and the devil were real. I talked to the church members, saying that the sermon was similar to what I experienced while dying. I spoke to approximately two hundred church members, and they applauded after I completed talking. After church, I had close to twenty people talking to me. They told me thank you for sharing my story. I was very proud and humbled in speaking to them. I wasn't nervous and was very confident to talk to a large crowd. It was a special strength that God gave me to be able to speak. I was always nervous when speaking in front of a large crowd in the past. I did the readings in church once a month. I became proud of myself for being able to read God's word.

I worked hard every day in rehabilitation, sometimes for almost two to three hours on weight lifting days. I would ride the recumbent bike and lift weights before a physical therapy session with Ryan once it started on the Tuesday after Thanksgiving. My goal was to get stronger so I could go back to work and maybe if I was lucky go late-season archery hunting with my crossbow that I purchased in August. I never intended to use a crossbow because I enjoyed using a recurve and compound bow. I was planning on using it for late-season muzzleloader or turkey season. I knew that eventually I would have to use a crossbow if my muscles weakened. I didn't expect to need to use the crossbow this hunting season. A doctor told me that I could hunt this year if I had somebody with me 100 percent of the time, didn't use a rifle or shotgun, only a crossbow, and if I got a deer, have another person drag it out. A shotgun, rifle, or muzzleloader would possibly break my ribs again and be too dangerous for my weak body.

I went scouting for deer from my truck where I could watch the fields and road. I saw some large bucks and plenty of does and fawns crossing the field or the road. I had to find a place to put a ground blind if I were able to hunt. I would have to be close to the road to have easy access and safety. I had been scouting about one week during the morning and evening.

I chose to put a ground blind about forty yards off the road. In the summer, Rick and I brush-hogged a path to a wild apple orchard. It was probably my best choice for me to stand in due to my physical condition. I would park my truck on the road and walk about eighty yards to the path.

My cousin Mark helped me set up the ground blind on Sunday, the day before the deer season. I wanted to set it up before Saturday, but my friend Dana was sick and couldn't help.

I went to rehabilitation, working very hard trying to get stronger. I was doing it for myself. I was only helping myself by doing as much as I could. The left side of my chest was still hurting very badly because I had a regression the Sunday after Thanksgiving and possibly pulled some muscles.

Unfortunately for me, I couldn't find anyone to hunt with for the morning because it was raining very hard and steady. In the evening, Dana hunted with me. I spotted six does that tried to sneak by, apparently looking for another hiding place. I eventually got too cold to stand and had to leave earlier than planned.

The second day I was able to hunt was Saturday, the last day. The temperature was well below freezing, around fifteen degrees. My friend Chuck hunted beside me. We stood for a couple of hours. Chuck had a badly sprained ankle, and I was still recovering, so neither one of us could handle the cold weather very well. My friend Chuck Larson spotted two deer at sunrise, but we both had crossbows, and they were out of range. My deer-hunting season ended without much success.

I continued my rehabilitation with Ryan. I also did my own exercising, such as riding the recumbent bike and leg lifts. Ryan had me walking on the treadmill and lifting weights. When I first started walking on the treadmill, which was used as a warm-up, I could barely walk 1 mile per hour. I continued working hard on the recumbent bike and treadmill. I made a lot of progress during my twelve-session rehabilitation. I was able to walk 3.6 miles per hour during my last session almost two months later.

Every day during my workout, I seemed to talk to someone new. Part of working out is often enhanced by talking to people and getting encouragement from them. I enjoyed every day talking to new people and sharing my story about going to heaven. Not all people were Christians. There were atheists and nonbelievers, yet they usually listened to my story. One man walked away when I asked him if I could share my story. I felt deeply hurt by having him walk away.

It was the first time that someone walked away from me. In a way, it was a lesson to me that not everybody would listen to my story. God gave me a chance to share the story with him, and the man did not accept it. It's not my job to have anyone accept my story. They have free will. All I can do is present my story to them.

Thanksgiving Day

Thanksgiving Day arrived after my fall from the tree stand. It was a day that I was really looking forward to. My niece Amy and her husband, Ryan, were hosting Thanksgiving dinner. Ryan was going to be my physical therapist, so we were going to talk about my schedule and goals to help me get stronger when we got some free time. I teased him and asked if he ever invited his other clients to dinner. Our session would start the Tuesday following Thanksgiving.

I bought a couple of gifts for Amy and Ryan's little boys, Ben and Landon. My nephew John and his wife, Kerri, were coming from North Carolina with their boys, Tyler and Aaron. When I was a little boy growing up, our parents bought us an Erector Set. It is a good toy to use your imagination and create things. I bought an Erector Set, two Trouble games, and two Pittsburgh Steelers, small footballs, for the boys.

Before I went to the dinner, I stopped at Our Lady of the Lake Church. I went in and prayed out loud to God, looking at the cross. This was something I started doing a few years ago in church. I look at the cross while praying the Our Father in church during the mass. I believe God wanted me to write in my book that He wants an end to abortion. I felt that God told me that abortion hurts Him deeply. I believe a miracle and a sign happened when I was leaving the church. On a bulletin board that was approximately two by three feet long, a picture of Mother Theresa stood out among all the other postings. It was as if it was the only posting because nothing else caught my attention. I looked at the picture of Mother Theresa, and beside it, this was written: "Abortion hurts everybody."

I went to the Thanksgiving dinner. After dinner, I brought out the toys and games. We played Trouble, and I established the rule to not touch the board unless it was your turn. If you touched the board, you would lose a turn. It's funny because I even lost a turn. I had Ben, Landon, and Tyler play. I let Aaron be my partner until he got bored. We had a great time! I told them that the only time they were ever allowed to get into trouble was if they opened the box to play the game. I wanted it to be a good example and a lesson also. We shared many laughs while playing, and the boys displayed great sportsmanship skills. I told them if they complained, they would lose a turn also.

I had the boys take out the erector set. They were very good at playing quietly and sharing. Landon brought up his toy that he built to show me. Ben made a dinosaur. I was very proud of the boys for cooperatively playing and sharing the erector set.

I watched football and played catch with the Pittsburgh Steelers football with Ben and Landon. The boys did a really good job listening to me when catching the ball. I was a receivers coach at Cochranton High School for ten years. I tried to make catching the football fun for the boys. They did a great job.

Later in the evening, I had Ben read a story to me about dinosaurs. I found out that he shared the same fascination with dinosaurs that I had as a young child. I told him that before 1980, there were only about two hundred dinosaurs discovered. In 2018, close to eight hundred dinosaurs had been discovered. I learned new dinosaurs as he read the book to me.

While talking to Ben, I asked him if he believed in God. He replied, "Yes, I believe in God." I was very touched and proud of him for his answer. Ben was only six and a half years old then.

I got the chance to tell my nephew John about my experience. We shared some stories in the past and relived some of the things we did while he was growing up, like when I coached him in football and hunted with him when he got his second deer.

At the end of the night, Ben ran to me and gave me a big hug and said goodbye. I felt it was so thoughtful of him.

What Was Heaven Like?

People have asked me what I experienced in heaven. What did I hear or see? Did I see God? What was heaven like? I didn't see God and my mom, but I heard their voices. I didn't see any pearly gates. I tell people I must have taken the back way in or a shortcut. I can describe heaven as a very beautiful place. I could see for miles. It seemed like, in the distance, I saw hills and mountains. It was like a beautiful sunrise without the sun. Heaven was very bright and colorful.

I didn't tell a lot of people, but the most amazing experience I had was meeting my little brother or sister that my mom had as a miscarriage before my sister, brothers, and I were born. I stood face-to-face with my sister who was never born. She was four or five years old in heaven! I recognized her right away as my sister. She didn't have a name because my mom and dad didn't know if the baby was a boy or girl.

She talked to me and welcomed me to heaven. She looked a lot like my sister Frances but with differences. She had shoulder-length hair and was about two or three inches shorter than me. I figured that I must have been about thirty-six to forty inches tall. My sister told me that I will be back in heaven again someday and that it wasn't my time yet.

Later, I talked to my sister Frances about her. I said, "Remember when mom told us that we have a brother or sister in heaven? Well, I saw our sister in heaven!"

Frances said, "I always thought we had a sister!"

I said, "Don't tell our brothers. They will have to go to heaven to find out!" Either that, or read my book! I told her that our sister stayed with me for a full week in the hospital as a spirit when I was getting better.

I later told my sister Frances that I wanted to name our sister. Because the doctors told my mom that she wasn't going to be able to have children, I picked out the name Sarah, like Abraham's wife, because she wasn't supposed to have children because she was barren. Frances said that I made a good choice for her name. I had the feeling that Sarah liked her name also.

Getting Better

I've had many people ask me if I have learned my lesson because I fell from my tree stand. I always reply, "Yes! God and heaven are real!" But what they really meant was that I need to use a safety harness and also make sure I use it while climbing up and down. I tell them that it was in God's plan to have me fall and be hurt. I believe that He wanted a spokesman to be brave enough to talk about God and heaven. Why did He pick me? I have always been kind of shy and reserved about speaking about God unless I knew the person well. I wasn't the man who now confidently talks to total strangers about falling from the tree stand and going to heaven.

I want to encourage hunters to use a safety harness while in a tree stand. As an International Bowhunter Education instructor, we have taught students to always use a safety harness when climbing up and down a tree. While in the tree stand, it is important to use the safety harness at all times. My friend Rick Uplinger fell out of his tree stand when a cable snapped. Rick was hurt badly and took four months to get better and return to work. When I bought my Timber Tall tree stand eleven years ago, I believed it was the safest stand in the market. I often would even fall asleep in the stand. I felt safe in the stand, although climbing down with the stand was sometimes difficult and dangerous. Most accidents occur when climbing up and down in the tree stand. I have met other people who fell from a tree stand during my rehabilitation.

Another important safety plan is to make sure someone knows where you will be hunting. At my age and family history, heart attacks run in my family at a young age. When I fell from my tree stand, nobody knew exactly where I was standing, and my phone had only 5 percent battery life. It is also important to keep your phone charged in case of an emergency or if help is needed. I am a single man and live alone. I was fortunate enough that I had two friends who knew where I lived. I called them and gave them directions into the woods on how they could find me.

When I am able to talk to people about my experience, I find it to be so uplifting for me. I share with them my struggles to become physically, emotionally, and mentally stronger. I had to endure a lot of pain from a total of eleven broken ribs, getting five from my fall, four from CPR, and two that happened while being taken care of in the hospital. Being turned over when I was being cleaned up and having my bedding changed was something I didn't look forward to. I spent my day lying on my back because of my injuries. I worried about what was going to happen to me. I felt so much helplessness, weakness, and fear that I may never live or even walk again.

The nurses and doctors took very good care of me as my body made its slow recovery. I imagined people who could be dying with similar fears. My biggest strength was that God gave me a 100 percent chance to live. I want to give hope to people with illnesses, death, and tragedy that God can dwell within their hearts and minds. In heaven, the pain and suffering will no longer be part of our lives. The doctors gave me a 5 percent chance to live and told my family that I was one of the ten sickest people in the UPMC hospital.

My friend Rick later told me that on his birthday, they thought I wouldn't make it through the night. God blessed me with the strength to continue life as He had planned for me. At the time of my slow recovery, I didn't have plans to write this book. I believe that God revealed His wishes through my heart, mind, and soul. God blessed me with the opportunity to share with others that God and heaven are real. I feel that I have to give glory to God and praise His name for the miracle that He performed, giving me an extended life on earth.

I reflect on my injuries. Many people tell me that I was very lucky. Yes, they are right about me being very lucky! I was falling headfirst backward. I couldn't see the ground. I could have died from my fall, broke my neck or back, and been paralyzed. I could have landed on my legs, breaking bones in my feet, ankles, or legs. I could have broken my skull or landed on my head, causing me to be mentally challenged for the rest of my life.

I was given an opportunity to walk again and try to regain my strength to attempt to do things I had always taken for granted in life. I wanted to get physically better so I would be able to go to work again with children or the autistic boy I worked with as a teacher's aide. I had to get stronger and faster mentally, physically, and emotionally to be able to do my job. I wanted to be able to hunt and play softball again. All these goals were the bases of how hard I was willing to work for rehabilitation. I thank God for keeping me from more serious injuries than I had sustained. There were times when I lived through scary situations not knowing what the outcome would be. I didn't know many things during my recovery that made me worry. I was always imagining the worst possible outcome. I needed to pray for God's strength and guidance to aid in my rehabilitation and recovery.

God transformed me into a man who has become more confident and opened the door for me to speak about Him. I was always a shy man who didn't talk to people who were total strangers about God. Now I share my story with them with confidence as He guides my thoughts and words.

I would talk to people at Walmart and other stores without hesitation. I would speak to people every day in the YMCA. How could it be that I could share my story so openly with others? I was blessed with a special gift from God, and I believe that my duty on earth now is to share my story with everyone who is willing to open their ears and listen.

When I was a little boy, my mom told me how a man came into her property and used the Lord's name in vain. One of God's Ten Commandments is this: "Thou shalt not use the name of the Lord thy God in vain." My mom said my grandmother told him not to use the God's name in vain and to get off the property.

It bothers me that movies and some media use the Lord's name in vain. A movie doesn't have to use this type of disrespect to God. Movies and media influence many people. This type of entertainment can cause people to let their guards down and accept this improper language into their vocabulary. When I hear this language, I tell people to please not use the Lord's name in vain around me.

In March, I went to a game dinner where Jimmy Sites was the speaker. I had never heard of Jimmy Sites before. He is the producer and host of *Spiritual Outdoor Adventures*. I took my cousin Mark and his grandson Jacob as my guests.

Jimmy was a very inspirational, funny, and good speaker. One of the things that he spoke about was movies and media using the Lord's name in vain. I am glad that I got to meet him because I agree with him. It is not necessary for movies and media to use the language. In my opinion, it doesn't make the movie better.

I was able to speak to Jimmy Sites after his show. I told him about my near-death experience. He told me that his mom also had a near-death experience. He asked me to let him know when my book is completed and comes out.

I want to be able to encourage people who have a life-threatening illness to find strength in God's love and compassion for us. In a way, I suffered many experiences that people are living with each and every day. My pain disappeared when I died. Unfortunately, when I came back to earth, it was severe again.

I want to encourage hunters and people to think about safety. Always use a safety harness when using a tree stand. Take time to check your equipment for any physical defects that might cause a malfunction. I had a man tell me that he replaces his tree stand with a new one every three or four years. Always be careful when loading or unloading a firearm. People ask me if I had learned a lesson. I should have had a safety harness on to be safe when climbing up or down in a tree. I learned that God and heaven are real!

I want to thank all the medical staff at Meadville Medical Center, Hamot, UPMC Presbyterian, and HealthSouth for taking care of me and helping me in my road to recovery. I want to thank my family and friends for their prayers and participation in my recovery. I eventually heard that ten churches were praying for me. I especially want to thank God for the blessing that He gave me: a chance to spread the word that God and heaven are real!

About the Author

Joseph Drda is a first-time author who grew up in Northwestern Pennsylvania. He enjoys many sports, including hunting, trapping, fishing, baseball, football, volleyball, and basketball. Joseph went to Slippery Rock University, graduating with a health and physical education degree. Later, he went to Edinboro University, graduating with an elementary education degree.

Joseph was a substitute teacher where he coached football, boys and girls basketball, boys and girls volleyball, and girls softball. He grew up in a Roman Catholic family with both mom and dad being Catholic. He has one sister and four brothers. He was an altar boy, serving God. As an adult, he became a member in his church's Holy Name Society, got elected as church council vice president, and became a lecturer. He volunteered as a supervisor for children in a local church to play games.

Joseph had enjoyed being in nature from a young age, learning about hunting, fishing, and trapping from his dad, uncles, and neighbor. His uncle got him interested in archery hunting, and he has harvested many deer and three wild turkeys with his bow.

He was an International Bowhunting Education instructor for seven years. As an instructor, he taught first aid, hunting techniques, and tree stand safety. Joseph also worked with physically and mentally challenged children and teenagers and volunteered for local and state special olympics. Currently, he works as a teacher's aide in a life skills classroom. He grew to appreciate children and adults with illnesses and handicaps with his experiences.